The Solar System

Robin Birch

Jupiter

CHELSEA CLUBHOUSE

An Imprint of Chelsea House Publishers
A Haights Cross Communications Company
Philadelphia

This edition first published in 2004 in the United States of America by Chelsea Clubhouse, a division of Chelsea House Publishers and a subsidiary of Haights Cross Communications.

Chelsea House Publishers
1974 Sproul Road, Suite 400
Broomall, PA 19008-0914

The Chelsea House world wide web address is www.chelseahouse.com

Library of Congress Cataloging-in-Publication Data Applied for.
ISBN 0-7910-7926-0

First published in 2004 by
MACMILLAN EDUCATION AUSTRALIA PTY LTD
627 Chapel Street, South Yarra, Australia, 3141

Associated companies and representatives throughout the world.

Edited by Anna Fern
Text and cover design by Cristina Neri, Canary Design
Illustrations by Melissa Webb
Photo research by Legend Images

Printed in China

Acknowledgements
The author and publisher are grateful to the following for permission to reproduce copyright material:

Cover photograph of Jupiter courtesy of Photodisc.

Art Archive, p. 4 (right); TSADO/NASA/Tom Stack/Auscape, pp. 14, 19; Digital Vision, pp. 26, 28; Calvin J. Hamilton, pp. 7, 10; Imageaddict, p. 11; Walter Myers/www.arcadiastreet.com, pp. 9, 24 (bottom); NASA/HST, p. 5 (top); NASA/JPL, p. 20 (right); NASA/JPL/Caltech, p. 15 (top left and right); NASA/JPL/John Hopkins University Applied Physics Laboratory, p. 16 (top); NASA/NSSDC, p. 24 (top); NASA/University of Arizona, p. 25; NASA/University of Arizona/LPL, p. 20 (left); Photodisc, pp. 12, 16 (bottom), 29; Photoessentials, p. 21; Photolibrary.com/SPL, pp. 4 (left), 6, 15 (bottom), 18, 27; Reuters, pp. 13, 22, 23.

Background and border images, including view of Jupiter, courtesy of Photodisc.

Please note
At the time of printing, the Internet addresses appearing in this book were correct. Owing to the dynamic nature of the Internet, however, we cannot guarantee that all these addresses will remain correct.

Contents

Glossary words

When you see a word printed in bold, **like this**, you can look up its meaning in the glossary on page 31.

Discovering Jupiter

The **planet** Jupiter looks like a bright **star** in the night sky. It is the fourth brightest object in the sky after the Sun, the Moon, and the planet Venus. If Jupiter is in the night sky, it may be there at any time of night.

People have known about Jupiter since **ancient** times. It is named after the king of the Roman gods, Jupiter. Jupiter's Greek name was Zeus, and his English name was Jove. The planet Jupiter was named after the king of the gods because it shines so brightly and moves slowly through the stars like a king.

▶ A painting showing the Roman god Jupiter launching his thunderbolts

▼ Jupiter in the night sky

Jupiter

The word "planet" means "wanderer." Stars always make the same pattern in the sky. Planets slowly change their location in the sky, compared to the stars around them. This is why planets were called "wanderers."

▲ The planet Jupiter, photographed from the *Hubble Space Telescope*

▶ This is the symbol for Jupiter.

Jupiter has four large moons **revolving** around it, in the same way Earth's Moon **orbits** Earth. These moons can only be seen with **binoculars** or a **telescope**. The moons were discovered by the Italian **astronomer** Galileo in the year 1610. Galileo found the first moons to be seen apart from our Earth's Moon.

Astronomers have used telescopes to study Jupiter from Earth since 1610. They could see bands of clouds on Jupiter which kept changing as they moved around the planet. The first close-up pictures of Jupiter were taken by the **space probe** *Pioneer 10,* in 1973.

The Fifth Planet

Jupiter is part of the solar system, which consists mainly of the Sun and nine planets. The planets revolve around the Sun. Jupiter is the fifth closest planet to the Sun.

The solar system also has comets and asteroids moving around in it. Comets are large balls of rock, ice, **gas**, and dust which orbit the Sun. Comets start their orbit far away from the Sun. They travel in close to the Sun, go around it, and then travel out again. When they come close to the Sun, comets grow a tail.

Asteroids are rocks. There are millions of asteroids in the solar system. They can be small or large. The largest asteroid, named Ceres, is about 584 miles (940 kilometers) across. Most asteroids orbit the Sun in a path called the asteroid belt, between the orbits of Mars and Jupiter.

▶ The solar system

The solar system is about 4,600 million years old.

The planets in the solar system are made of rock, ice, gas, and liquid. Mercury, Venus, Earth, and Mars are made of rock. Pluto is probably made of rock and ice. These are the smallest planets.

Jupiter, Saturn, Uranus, and Neptune are made mainly of gas and liquid. They are the largest planets. They are often called the gas giants, because they have no solid ground to land on.

Planets, comets, and asteroids are lit up by light from the Sun. They do not make their own light the way stars do.

▶ The planets, from smallest to largest, are: Pluto, Mercury, Mars, Venus, Earth, Neptune, Uranus, Saturn, and Jupiter.

Planet	Average distance from Sun	
Mercury	35,960,000 miles	(57,910,000 kilometers)
Venus	67,190,000 miles	(108,200,000 kilometers)
Earth	92,900,000 miles	(149,600,000 kilometers)
Mars	141,550,000 miles	(227,940,000 kilometers)
Jupiter	483,340,000 miles	(778,330,000 kilometers)
Saturn	887,660,000 miles	(1,429,400,000 kilometers)
Uranus	1,782,880,000 miles	(2,870,990,000 kilometers)
Neptune	2,796,000,000 miles	(4,504,000,000 kilometers)
Pluto	3,672,300,000 miles	(5,913,520,000 kilometers)

The name "solar system" comes from the word "Solaris." This is the official name for the Sun. The Sun is a star.

As it travels around the Sun, the huge planet Jupiter spins on its **axis**.

Rotation and Revolution

Jupiter **rotates** on its axis once every 9.83 Earth hours. This is a very fast spin for such a huge planet. Because Jupiter's axis is in an almost upright position, Jupiter does not have seasons like some other planets do. Jupiter's fast rotation affects its shape, which is slightly flat at the top and bottom, and wider across the middle.

Jupiter takes 11.86 Earth years to revolve around the Sun once, which is the length of Jupiter's year. Jupiter's orbit is almost a perfect circle. The Sun's **gravity** keeps Jupiter revolving around it.

Sun

Axis

Day

Night

◀ Jupiter rotating on its axis, revolving around the Sun

▲ Compare the size of Jupiter and Earth.

Jupiter is made mainly of the substance hydrogen, like stars are. If Jupiter was about 50 times heavier, it could possibly turn into a star.

Size

Jupiter is the largest of all the planets. It is 88,793 miles (142,984 kilometers) in **diameter**, which is about 11 times wider than Earth. Jupiter is also the heaviest planet—it is more than twice as heavy as all the other planets combined. Jupiter's **mass** is about 318 times the mass of Earth.

Jupiter is about the largest size that a planet can be. If more substance was added to Jupiter, it would not get larger. Instead, the substance would be squeezed together more tightly.

Structure

Jupiter is made up of about 75 percent hydrogen and 25 percent helium. There are also very small amounts of the substances methane, water, ammonia, sulfur, and carbon dioxide, as well as some rock.

Jupiter most likely has a small core made of rock, surrounded by ices. The rock may be a very thick liquid, or it may be solid. Although the core is small compared to the size of Jupiter, it is larger than Earth. The temperature of the core is probably about 36,000 degrees Fahrenheit (20,000 degrees Celsius).

▼ Inside Jupiter. The boundaries between the layers are not as clear as shown here—there is a gradual change from one layer to the next.

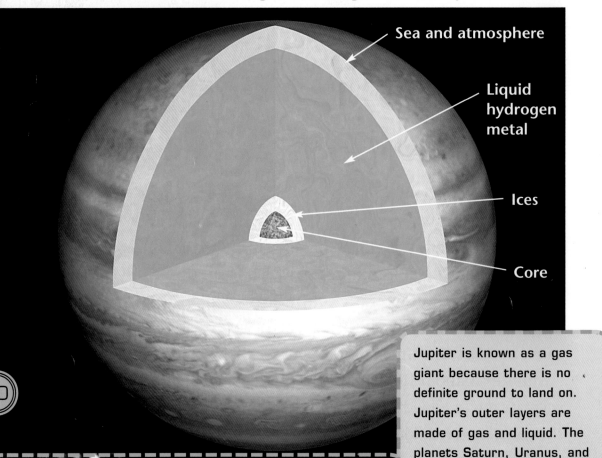

Sea and atmosphere

Liquid hydrogen metal

Ices

Core

Jupiter is known as a gas giant because there is no definite ground to land on. Jupiter's outer layers are made of gas and liquid. The planets Saturn, Uranus, and Neptune are also gas giants.

▶ This mercury is a liquid metal. A similar liquid hydrogen metal is found inside Jupiter, but is not found naturally on Earth.

Around Jupiter's core is a wide layer of liquid metal which makes up most of the planet. The liquid metal is made of the substance hydrogen. This layer is cooler than the core. Its temperature is about 20,000 degrees Fahrenheit (11,000 degrees Celsius).

Liquid hydrogen and helium form a sea around the outside of Jupiter's liquid metal layer. This sea is about 12,000 miles (20,000 kilometers) deep. On the outside of Jupiter is a layer of hydrogen and helium gas, about 600 miles (1,000 kilometers) thick. This layer is Jupiter's **atmosphere**.

Clouds

Jupiter has colored bands of clouds across it which can be seen from Earth through a small telescope. The darker-colored bands are called belts. The lighter-colored bands are known as zones. Space probes have taken close-up pictures of Jupiter which show that these clouds are orange, brown, red, cream, and white.

The cloud bands are blown around Jupiter by high-speed winds. Bands next to each other often blow in opposite directions. The winds are caused by heat from the Sun, and by heat from deep inside Jupiter.

▼ Jupiter's clouds form bands.

Winds on Jupiter reach 200 to 300 miles (300 to 500 kilometers) per hour.

The colors of Jupiter's clouds may be caused by the sulfur in them, which may have turned different shades of red, orange, and yellow.

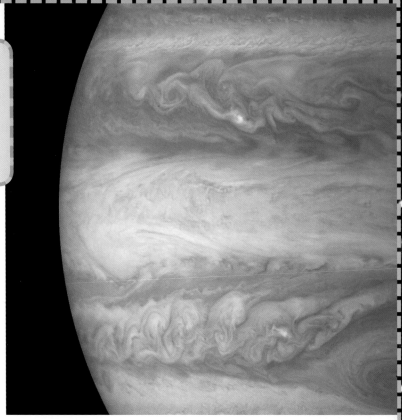

▲ Clouds on Jupiter

There are three main layers of clouds on the very outside of Jupiter. The top layer has very tiny **crystals** of ammonia ice. The layer below has a substance made from ammonia combined with sulfur. The bottom layer of cloud has water drops and crystals of water ice, like the clouds on Earth.

The colors of the clouds may all be in the top ammonia layer. In this case, we would be seeing just the upper layer when we look at Jupiter. However, we may be seeing colored lower layers showing through gaps in the upper layers, which may be white.

Storms

On the southern **hemisphere** of Jupiter there is a huge storm cloud known as the Great Red Spot. This storm has been raging for at least 100 years. It may have been seen more than 300 years ago by people studying Jupiter with telescopes. The storm cloud is usually red, but sometimes it turns orange or pink.

The Great Red Spot is an oval-shaped whirlpool of cloud about 16,000 miles (25,000 kilometers) long and 7,000 miles (12,000 kilometers) wide. It is so large that three Earths could fit on it. The Great Red Spot is colder and higher up than the clouds around it.

▼ The Great Red Spot

The Great Red Spot turns around on itself, taking a few days to turn once. It turns in a counterclockwise direction. It also races around the planet, swallowing up other storms.

▲ A white oval and swirls of cloud   ▲ White ovals

▶ A brown oval

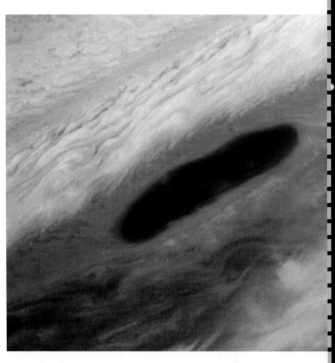

Often the cloud bands next to each other blow in opposite directions around Jupiter. When they come up against each other, the clouds swirl around into wavy patterns and whirlpools.

There are many storm clouds similar to the Great Red Spot on Jupiter, but smaller, which come and go from time to time. There are also many small, white, oval clouds on Jupiter. Each one is a giant storm. There are also brown ovals on Jupiter. The storms are full of thunder and lightning, rain and snow.

Magnetic Field

Jupiter has a very strong **magnetic field** in parts of space around it which is 10 times stronger than Earth's magnetic field. Planets with magnetic fields are huge magnets. Jupiter's magnetic field is caused by the liquid hydrogen metal inside it, which spins as the planet spins, making the magnetic field.

Jupiter's magnetic field traps **charged** particles floating in space. These charged particles can interfere with the electronics of spacecraft approaching Jupiter. They sometimes cause **auroras** at the north and south **poles** of Jupiter.

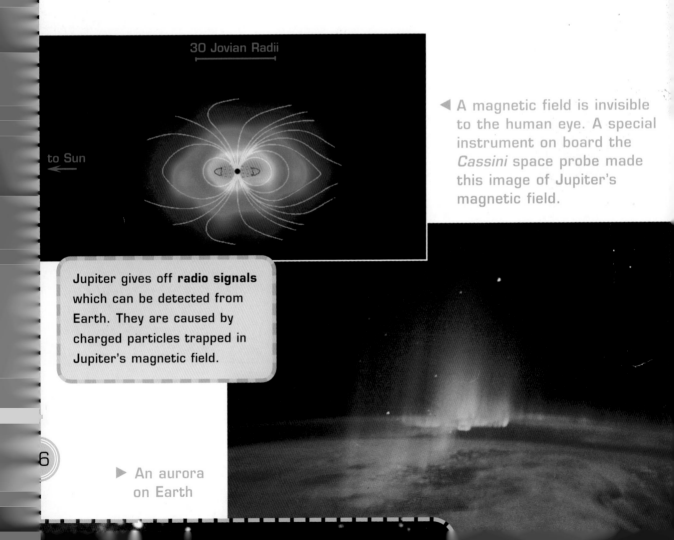

30 Jovian Radii

to Sun

◀ A magnetic field is invisible to the human eye. A special instrument on board the *Cassini* space probe made this image of Jupiter's magnetic field.

Jupiter gives off **radio signals** which can be detected from Earth. They are caused by charged particles trapped in Jupiter's magnetic field.

▶ An aurora on Earth

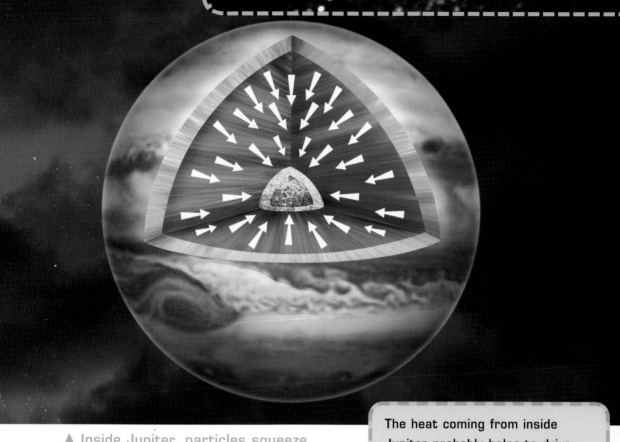

▲ Inside Jupiter, particles squeeze inwards and produce heat.

The heat coming from inside Jupiter probably helps to drive the fast winds in the atmosphere. This would help cause the cloud patterns on the surface.

Giving off Heat

The temperature at the top of Jupiter's clouds is –240 degrees Fahrenheit (–150 degrees Celsius). This is not as cold as we would expect Jupiter to be, when it is so far away from the Sun. Jupiter gives off more heat than it receives from the Sun, so it must make heat of its own.

Astronomers believe that Jupiter's heat is made deep inside the planet. They think that the substances inside Jupiter are being slowly squeezed together, because of Jupiter's very strong gravity. When the particles are pushed together like this, they heat up.

Moons and Rings

Jupiter has at least 58 moons circling around it, as well as rings of dust.

Moons

Jupiter has four large moons and many small ones. The four large moons of Jupiter were the first moons belonging to another planet ever to be seen. Their names are: Io, Europa, Ganymede, and Callisto.

Jupiter's four large moons were discovered by Galileo, in 1610. One night, looking through the telescope he had built, Galileo saw what looked like three small stars next to Jupiter. A week later, he had found four of them. Galileo noticed that these objects stayed near Jupiter, and guessed that he had found four moons. The moons could not be seen without the telescope. The four large moons are now known as the Galilean moons.

▼ Jupiter and its four large moons, as they appear through a small telescope

Galileo

Galileo Galilei was one of the first people to build a telescope to study stars and planets. He was born in Italy in 1564 and became a mathematician and philosopher.

▲ Jupiter and the Galilean moons

Jupiter has many smaller moons. Twenty-three of them have been given names. More moons have been discovered, making at least 58 moons altogether. The Internet has up-to-date information on discoveries of moons—some web sites are listed on page 30.

Jupiter has four small moons closer to it than the four large moons. These inner moons are between 79,000 and 138,000 miles (128,000 and 222,000 kilometers) away from Jupiter. It is probably dust from the inner moons which has caused Jupiter's rings.

The rest of Jupiter's moons, called outer moons, are small. They are between 6,889,000 and 18,630,000 miles (11,094,000 and 30,000,000 kilometers) from Jupiter. Many outer moons were probably passing asteroids which were caught by Jupiter's strong gravity.

Io

Io is the closest large moon to Jupiter. Its orbit is 262,000 miles (422,000 kilometers) from Jupiter. Io is 2,255 miles (3,632 kilometers) in diameter.

Io's colorful orange and yellow surface is caused by **volcanoes**. Orange and yellow sulfur pours out of the volcanoes, and spreads out over the ground. These volcanoes were the very first active volcanoes to be found on another planet or its moon by a spacecraft. Black lakes of **lava** are found here and there over Io's surface. White snow made of sulfur dioxide also comes out of the volcanoes and falls to the ground.

The volcanoes on Io are probably caused by the gravities of Jupiter and the moon Europa, which pull on the liquids inside Io. Jupiter's strong magnetic field probably stirs up the liquids inside Io, too.

▼ Io

▲ This picture of Io shows a volcano erupting on the horizon.

▼ Europa

In Greek myths, Io was a young woman loved by the god Zeus (Jupiter). Europa was a princess kidnapped by Zeus, and taken to Crete.

Europa

About 417,000 miles (671,000 kilometers) from Jupiter is Europa, the second large moon. Europa is 1,941 miles (3,126 kilometers) in diameter.

Europa has the smoothest surface of all the moons in the solar system. The surface is a thin layer of ice, probably up to 6 miles (10 kilometers) thick, which makes a crust around Europa. Europa is the brightest of Jupiter's large moons, because the ice reflects the sunlight.

Europa's icy crust has long cracks in it, and the surface has a few impact **craters** made by asteroids. Europa seems to have an ocean of liquid water below the crust. When the crust gets broken, this water would fill the gaps and freeze, making the crust smooth again.

Ganymede

About 664,000 miles (1,070,000 kilometers) from Jupiter is Ganymede, the third large moon. Its diameter is 3,276 miles (5,276 kilometers). Ganymede is the largest moon in the solar system. It is about the size of the planet Mercury.

Ganymede is made of about half rock and half water or ice. It probably has a rocky core surrounded mainly by ice. The ice on the surface is dirty, giving much of Ganymede a darkish color. The oldest parts of the surface are the darkest color. The parts of the surface with fresh ice are white. Liquids have come through cracks in the crust and frozen, making new icy crust.

◀ Ganymede

Ganymede has a very large dark area called Galileo Regio. This can be seen from Earth with telescopes.

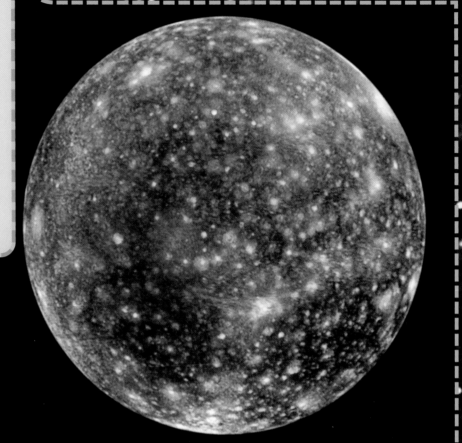

▶ Callisto

Callisto

Callisto is the farthest of the large moons from Jupiter, orbiting 664,000 miles (1,070,000 kilometers) away. Callisto is 2,990 miles (4,820 kilometers) in diameter—slightly smaller than Ganymede. It has a crust made of ice and rock. It probably has water or ice under the crust, and a core made of rock.

Callisto is covered with impact craters. It is the most thickly cratered object in the solar system found so far. The craters have been made by asteroids hitting Callisto. The newest craters are white, where fresh ice is showing. The largest crater is called Valhalla Basin.

Rings

In photographs, Jupiter does not appear to have rings around it. Rings were discovered by the space probe *Voyager 1* in 1979. It was a huge surprise to most astronomers at the time.

Jupiter's rings are dark, unless the sunlight catches them in a certain way, and they are much smaller than Saturn's rings. Jupiter's rings are made of very dark grains of rock. They do not seem to have any pieces of ice in them, like Saturn's rings. Ice would make the rings brighter, because it would reflect the sunlight.

Voyager 1 only discovered Jupiter's rings because two astronomers insisted it should look for them after going all that way. Other astronomers thought it would be a waste of time, but they were wrong.

▲ The rings of Saturn (top) are highly visible compared to the rings of Jupiter (right).

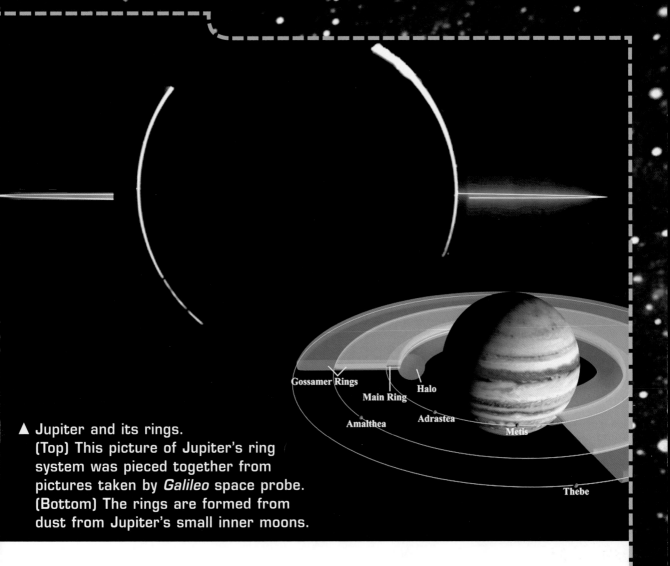

Gossamer Rings

Main Ring

Halo

Amalthea

Adrastea

Metis

Thebe

▲ Jupiter and its rings.
(Top) This picture of Jupiter's ring system was pieced together from pictures taken by *Galileo* space probe.
(Bottom) The rings are formed from dust from Jupiter's small inner moons.

Jupiter has one ring with three major parts. The rings come from dust blown off Jupiter's tiny inner moons, when asteroids hit them. The moons give the rings a constant supply of new dust.

The major part of Jupiter's ring, called the main ring, is flattened, like Saturn's rings. The main ring is about 4,000 miles (7,000 kilometers) wide. Its dust probably comes from the inner moons Metis and Adrastea. Inside the main ring there is a cloud-like ring called the halo ring. Just outside the main ring is a faint see-through ring called the gossamer ring.

Exploring Jupiter

Jupiter has been visited by several spacecraft without people on board. The spacecraft were operated by astronomers on Earth by sending and receiving radio signals. These types of spacecraft are called space probes.

The space probe *Pioneer 10* was the first to visit Jupiter, in 1973. *Pioneer 11* visited Jupiter in 1974, then flew on to Saturn. The Pioneers were sent to test whether space probes could survive flying through the asteroid belt and Jupiter's magnetic field. They took close-up photographs of Jupiter and its moons and gathered information about Jupiter's magnetic field.

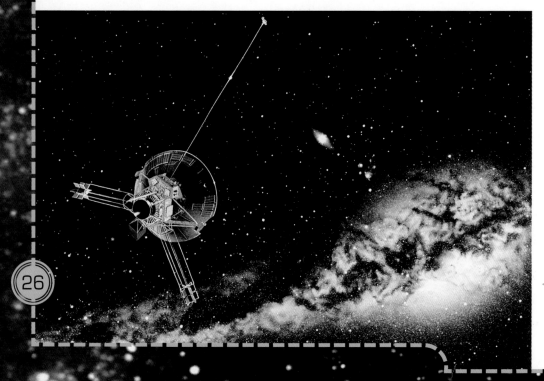

◀ The space probe *Pioneer 10*

▲ *Voyager* space probe

Voyager 1 and *Voyager 2*

The space probes *Voyager 1* and *Voyager 2* visited Jupiter in 1979. *Voyager 1* flew on to Saturn, and *Voyager 2* flew on to visit Saturn, Uranus, and Neptune.

The two Voyagers found lightning and auroras on Jupiter. They observed how the gases and clouds moved around and showed that the Great Red Spot rotated on itself in a counterclockwise direction. The Voyagers discovered Jupiter's rings. They also discovered the volcanoes on Io, and the detailed appearances of the other three large moons around Jupiter. The Voyagers discovered three of Jupiter's four inner moons: Adrastea, Metis, and Thebe.

Galileo

Galileo was the first space probe sent to orbit Jupiter, rather than just fly past. It was launched in 1989, and arrived at Jupiter in 1995. It sent a **probe** into Jupiter's atmosphere. The atmosphere probe beamed observations back to Earth, then was crushed by the atmosphere. *Galileo*'s **orbiter** continued on until 2003. It has changed the way astronomers understand Jupiter's rings, and discovered possible oceans underneath Callisto and Europa.

Hubble Space Telescope

The *Hubble Space Telescope (HST)* has taken excellent photographs of Jupiter. The *HST* is a telescope which orbits Earth, in space. It gets a clearer view of space than telescopes on Earth because it is above the atmosphere.

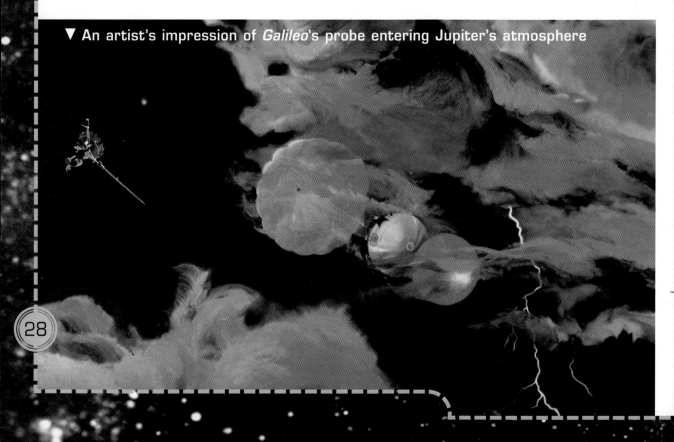

▼ An artist's impression of *Galileo*'s probe entering Jupiter's atmosphere

▼ The *Hubble Space Telescope* above Earth

Questions about Jupiter

There is still a lot to learn about Jupiter. One day, astronomers hope to find out the answers to questions such as these:

- How deep down inside Jupiter do the winds blow? What really drives the winds so hard and so fast?

- Storms do not usually last for hundreds of years—why has the Great Red Spot lasted so long?

- What really causes the colors in Jupiter's clouds? Are we seeing the top layer of the clouds, or lower layers showing through gaps in upper layers?

- What causes the volcanoes on the moon Io?

- How thick is the ice crust on Europa? Is there really an ocean of water under the crust?

- What has made the long cracks on Europa?

Jupiter Fact Summary

Distance from Sun (average)	483,340,000 miles (778,330,000 kilometers)
Diameter (at equator)	88,793 miles (142,984 kilometers)
Mass	317.89 times Earth's mass
Density	1.33 times the density of water
Gravity	2.36 times Earth's gravity
Temperature (top of clouds)	–240 degrees Fahrenheit (–150 degrees Celsius)
Rotation on axis	9.83 Earth hours
Revolution around Sun	11.86 Earth years
Number of moons	58 plus

Web Sites

quest.arc.nasa.gov/galileo/index.html
NASA's Galileo mission, online from Jupiter

www.nineplanets.org/
The nine planets—a tour of the solar system

www.enchantedlearning.com
Enchanted Learning web site—click on "Astronomy"

stardate.org
Stargazing with the University of Texas McDonald Observatory

pds.jpl.nasa.gov/planets/welcome.htm
Images from NASA's planetary exploration program

Glossary

ancient from thousands of years ago

astronomer a person who studies stars, planets, and other bodies in space

atmosphere a layer of gas around a large body in space

auroras curtains or bands of light in the sky

axis an imaginary line through the middle of an object, from top to bottom

binoculars an instrument with two eye pieces, for making far away objects look bigger and more detailed

charged carrying electric energy

constellation an area of sky which has certain stars in it

craters bowl-shaped hollows in the ground

crystals tiny pieces of pure substance

density a measure of how heavy something is for its size

diameter the distance across

gas a substance in which the particles are far apart, so they are not solid or liquid

gravity a force which pulls one body towards another body

hemisphere half of a globe

lava hot liquid rock which comes from out of the ground

magnetic field an area which affects magnets

mass a measure of how much substance is in something

orbiter a spacecraft which only travels around a body

orbits travels on a path around another body in space

planet a large body which circles the Sun

poles the top and bottom of a globe

probe a small spacecraft which travels down to or into a body

radio signals invisible rays

revolving traveling around another body

rotates spins

space probe a spacecraft which does not carry people

star a huge ball of glowing gas in space

telescope an instrument for making far away objects look bigger and more detailed

volcanoes holes in the ground through which lava flows

Index